The Sapling Raft Almanac

Todd M. Brown

Dedication

For my kids
They saved me from myself.

T.M.B.
9/29/2020

Banshee

You will never break through
Unless you do it in danger
With all of your demons whispering in your ear
And all that is left
Are those who dare.

Follow

I see the archipelagoes
Like volcanic stepping stones.

Make your way across the ocean.
Leave a wake
Underwater-
A way we can follow-
And I will follow.

You must facilitate your own escape.
Leave after sunset
And live in darkness
With the price you pay
For your disguise.

When you find the New World
Will that world see through you?
Will it find the outline?
Can you pass as your own master
If you've come wrapped in chains?

We can always add the whole thing back together
And return by the same way we came;
But here-
Suspended between worlds
Is the only place
I've ever found my true name.

Invocation

It seems
The only score I can settle
Is my own.
I can always frame
Another apology and repent;
You see-
I try to follow
But the instruments
Are too fragile.
They fail to fossilize,
Leaving only a trail
Of stars.
And what else am I to follow?
You murder the faithful
By the million
And allow a madman like me
To run free.
So, I tried everything
Until I found love
In anarchy.
Everybody has to freak out somehow.

Wait

I'm re-arranging
The same scratches
With the idea
I'll see the world in a new way.
All of the lies
These little marks were intended to be-
Will be.
The hope
Was always pinned like a note to my sleeve
With wistful beliefs.

We could have easily accepted
The hallowed emptiness
And pathetic craven gods
Of lick spittle,
Casual beliefs.

Are you coming through?

Make me believe-
These rituals of swine
And cruelty.
Make me believe
In one mighty storm.
Give us this reckoning
Of flesh eating gods
At the beckoning
Of mortally wounded man.

Make me believe.
Show us who you are-
Who you
Can never be.

The Arrangement of Land and Tide

What do we do now
To avoid answers?
We steer clear of many questions
And shape ourselves
Into tighter levels
Of domestication.
This comfort
Is the soft escape of creation,
And generations
Of regret.

At last, ask-
What do we get?

The ability to survive-
Alone,
And far behind enemy lines.

Always crooked
With our purpose
Ill defined,
Or self destruction by design.
We are able to follow
Close now- close enough.
One day soon,
We hope to kill a few
From the other side-
Of this strange arrangement
Between land
And tide.
There are things they can't turn back from,
Re-spawn, or start again
As metal minds
And so much cold dead weight.
Soon,

We can have a little place
In the sand,
Or below the surface of the moon.
Here we defy fate,
Learn to fly-
Sail away.

Premonition of the Fall of Western Civilization

Weeks went by-
I wouldn't go outside
Until sundown;
Drawing the shades,
Dimming the lights
Before they ate me alive.
Under siege-
Deliberations are always until dawn-
Or in jail.
And paranoia- the accusation
Of sights returned through the veil.
I asked, often- for the end;
The end of these hemispheres,
Pole reversal,
And the electrical impulse of the earth I once welcomed.
They blink, and then pause- and that's the end of it all.
The map of civilization lies buried outside the limitations of
watermarks
And scratches of blood on dyed papyrus and stretched animal hide.
We are held together by history
And history is held together by a crumbling frame.
So- there isn't much I'd choose to remember.
I lived in a warehouse
Stacked with weapons of wicked design,
And thousands of contained little expressions of feet per second.
If I needed them,
There would be no point in using them.
And I viewed life suspiciously
Until I found a suitably safe place to die.
This was the diversion
Of living and breathing
And confusion- juggling and jumping through their rings.
This idea-
That all is revealed

In the end.
So, save all of your money
For a nice plot
And a pauper's grave.
Convince me-
And my method of disbelief,
That life
Lies mummified inside this coffin-
Convince me
That I'm dying to survive.

Autumn Equinox

Bricked up windows
Have grown painted wings
Within the black mold outlines
Of indoor weather
And the artificial sun of light emitting diodes- sing.
Never what we are,
Or what we dreamed we could be.

When I was a child
I believed in the difference
Between darkness
And the shade
Of tall trees.

Fall-
Is falling down
And Autumn-
Halloween,
When we were children,
Inviolate of faith and translucent
Liquid dreams.

Now, do you see
What you believe?
You are here-
With me-
Playing in dead leaves
And flexible seasons-
Our fallible,
Stillborn spring.
We've taken every precaution
And been given this terrible thing.
They were alive in our minds
And now they are gone
As if they were nothing.

Only those feeling this loss
Understand this perfect little thing
That never was,
And why we give the dead
Our names;
That, seasons heal the loss they bring,
And wells are dug by the spring.

The Glass on the Beach

There are too few
New things
To see.
There are flames and survivors,
And the lies
Of how they came to be.
But, I like to look for fossils
And shells
Along the beach,
Where the glass reflects cosmology.
The dead
Are everything
The living claim to be.
The years of preservation
Are endearing,
And death itself-
Liberty,
Though, I am sorry to say it-
Even sorry to think it.
The words are wishes
When spoken,
And broken-
With entire trees now washed upon the shore.
And the cargo cult
Takes these offerings
Through the reach of these currents-
To which we pray for glass beads,
Blue jeans, and fatal heart disease.
Write it all down and come find us,
Then forget everything you wanted to say.
This is nothing-
It never mattered anyway.
All is dream,
All is sleep,
And you are nearly awake-

So, awake.

If the Master is Dead are we Free?

We all hear those whispers-
And singing,
Talking us into derelict corners
To claw at crumbling walls.

There- you can hear me?
Here- can you can see me, when the chemicals are kicking in
Through the twisted tales
Of insane history.

I know you are here;
As you exhale,
I breathe every little thing you've ever said.
It's in the air, all around me.

Do you see those shapeless ceiling stains?
Watch them,
Make them become clouds.
Turn them into storms
Where these walls are shorn
To the foundation
Of that wretched childhood home.
Let yourself out to track the wild creatures
You always wanted to be.

And like them,
We will be hunted
And broken to another's needs.

So, we stick to the shadows-
The shade of our salvation
Bringing blood offerings
By our own bleeding hands
And the blisters on our feet.
It's time to run away-

The beginning
Is not where the end
Lies down to die.
It is where we bury our Master
And turn our eyes to the sea.

Luna

What seed must grow
To gather unto itself
The lives below?

When daylight is blood
And the Sun must be drained,
The brethren bloom in darkness
And by dawn
The colors fade.

If there is nothing here,
I've no one but myself to blame.
What I believed to be pride,
Was fear,
And imagination
Was the lifetime of wind.
It is here
I watch and I listen.

If I fail
To deliberately set sail,
I'll be returned straight away
By the sea.
Turning back
Is giving in
To the worst kind of enemy.

I'm catching up
With the weather and fleeting time
To find purpose.
They all say:
Go now, if you would survive.
Drag death by what pale thread
You have left,
If you think dying

Would ease your mind.

So, I gathered everything I could carry-
On the shore
I left it behind.

The Scavenger

The next day I dream.
I wake
To someone selling pictures
And portraits of the children
We hoped to have.
The names of daydreams
In a landscape-
Miscarried,
And a place
Now covered by a city.
Methodical emptiness-
Like photo negatives
At the bottom of an otherwise empty envelope.
The pictures are gone- thrown away.
The cities are in ruins.
Have these ruins
Infected me?
I have nothing left to trade
But my escape,
And I am relieved
I've settled into the sea.
Behind me I see the smoke-
I'm not sure if I can believe-
As they will always be strangers,
All these people I see,
And open arms- a mystery.

When night falls, we see the flames.
With me are the many Gods
Of earth and air,
Wood and stream.
They say and do nothing,
Though I sense them listening.
I speak to them-
And they watch over me.

You get what you give-
If you earn it, you can eat.
Some flower,
Some bear fruit-
Some learn to live in between.

One

I'd become incapable of belief
And banished the idea
Of the one God
From my conscience.

I would define my life by simple actions
And short
Incomplete sentences
Recited alone,
Along the tops
Of sprawling mountain chains-
Traced with a fingertip
On the sky.
I pushed the idea of home
To the side.
I scrawl letters into the surface of the ocean
And erase them forever
In the wake.
I came here with nothing.
And nothing
Will I take.

Echoes

Across the ocean
Great continents rattle free,
To become islands
Independently.
Within all things,
An echo in tune-
Unexceptional and as tired
As perfection
Must be.
The world I left
Still rings in my head,
Until I speak with the open sea.
There is nothing to catch the words
Until the rain
Catches up with me.
It pulls them into the water,
Where they dissolve all questions,
The same
As the waves
Turn mountains into sand.
Answers are too far below,
Too far to ever know
Who we are in the present time.
We will never see
All the past
Put to sleep,
Beneath my sapling raft
Lies the past-
Exalting in mystery:
The ancient ruins on the shelf,
The seed
And magic reef.

Lighthouse

No one enters your life
While you wait.
No patient hands
To steady uncertain steps.
No wise advice
At just the right time.

There is nothing to save you
Or salvage your best intentions.

This overlord of time asks for nothing;
No excuses
Or explanations
Contrived along the way.
Neither is there an answer
Or interest
In mumbling about on the knees.

The map is the moon,
The sky,
And the stars,
Weaving a path
And an ambush
Behind your heart.
And you still listen to your heart,
Don't you?
You can't give it up.
Forever, beside yourself-
And I know because I am the same.
The water here is shallow
And the shore is near,
But, the anchor drags
Over the absence of mankind.
At another abandoned harbor
Only weathered pylons

Are left of the pier,
And a sign that says:
Welcome!
There is nothing here
But a guest book
And a broken pencil
Hanging by a thread.
I write nothing, and search for my name, instead.

Kingdom

Travel along the boundary
Between the world
And most days.
It becomes more difficult
To escape the box
We have been convinced
To build around ourselves
Since birth.
And would you,
If you could?
Or find something smaller-
Airtight,
And redundant by design?
A nice short leash
To wrap yourself around a tree
And ramble on about freedom-
The divine spark
And perfect separation
Between the things we almost believe.
Ours, is an alien world now-
The sounds become suspicious
And the voices incite violence,
Driven by anxiety, love, and silence.

A solitary flame,
A flicker-
If you watch,
You will see through these games.
Smile-
Spit back in their face.
You have the secret.
You have crushed the ore and mastered the flame.
Now, pull the sword from the stone,
And begin the Iron Age.

Tetragrammaton

I sleep now to dream-
To rewrite the world
And paint the sky to cover the seams.

Force thoughts into words
And wait for the voices to form.
Go back to the beginning;
Recite bedtime stories
With demons and dragons
And the battle for all souls.

Allow the survivors to escape,
Spread the story-
Grow old,
Navigate.
Those who rule
Over divides of mind
Have thus divided
Themselves in kind.
To create is imagination,
As to inspire
Is fertilization,
And tears-
The torment of rain.
Have you guarded the seed?
Have you prepared the soil,
Or harvested the bitter weeds?
There is no return of time-
The future is so far away,
Manifold at the face,
And open between worlds.
Here, is the Hall of Records.
It is here we realize
We have been born inside-
A fractal of one mind.

You may carry nothing
But that inside.
You must earn the kingdom
To be given the key,
And knowledge-
When you have become its repository.

Effigy

The sun on the water
No longer hurts my eyes,
Whether bitter
Or blind,
Or a lifetime
Ignorant of the spectrum of true light.

I've just gotten used
To all the secrets
I'm determined to keep-
The silence I've resigned myself to be.
What little there is worth saying
Is short the amputation
Of run on escapades.

The old worlds are divided,
Sacked,
And struggling to survive.
On every doorstep
Is regret
And everything I failed to forgive.
An elaborate straw man
In effigy-
Every savior scrounged up
To inflict fear
And hustle donations
For a nice vacation
This year.

Vessel

The replications take the shape
Of their containers,
Yet you remain shaken,
Yourself unsettled-
Hoping someone or something
Is in charge.
Something that will forgive them
And preserve this clay model
Of a soul
Given to a deity
To resurrect their own.

We began as hunters
And hatred,
Our lost children.
They were told this was holy ground-
And they gathered seeds
Until civilization
Could be sown
Among the weeds and thorns
Of wandering blame.
And by sin- if you call it that,
These tangles trip and follow
Until some other excuses can be made.

Between the walls of this fortress
The gaslight corridors exchange
This trust
In cunning
And the hunt of innocent game.

Leaves

There are long days
And overgrown trails
Through the old strange ways.

Inside,
The shadows in the corner fold together
And wind themselves up in my pockets
Like the soft letters of first love,
Opened again
And re-read.

And I collect them,
Because I can't bring myself to throw them away-
These foreign coins
Are the currency
Of those days
And the costume that came with the stage.

I organize them by nation
By date
By color
By weight-
It is the deepest part of the program,
The part I am trying to erase:
That I gather these crumbling leaves
And record them as evidence
To the last will
And testament
Of trees,

And the forest I leave
Behind me.

I pack it all in boxes
And keep them
In the back of the closet
With everything else
I allowed to chase me away.
They are pressed between the pages.
I exchange them for today.

ZepTepi

Everything seems softer around the edges
And in the back of my mind.
The only sound
Is the water
Inching forward in time-
Into dawn,
And into the sun- keeping the corona behind all eyes,
Illuminating things in the darkness
I've never known to be there.
That distant mind I'd recognized
As the master,
Was only mine.
Where ever I go on this battlefield
I find the front lines
Are redrawn behind me,
With the hope I will surrender.
The sky-
The sea and I-
Retreat
Towards dusk at the end of this tunnel,
Complete, within my life-
One small victory
In a world of defeat
And lies.
The shadows of what I have always wanted to be-
Planned to be-
Failed to be-
Overtake the apparition of what is,
And all that's left of this dream.
I'm grateful to the distant mind,
Distorting time and eyes,
Accustomed to the darkness and the impression
Of where there be monsters
Along the edge of this earth.
A nice trap

Set by those who made the maps
Of the new world-
Secret for centuries-
The invisible shackles
Of fear and uncertainty.

Now, we are free.

Scribe

Superstitions live on
As trauma goes from its first steps
To the stage
And on to what the scribe behind the curtain will say.

Love, not in passing,
But in desperation,
And know well
Those things we carved into ourselves.
From all this,
We put the first script into print.
The blood of this loving impression,
Our generational infection,
And the only question:
How can we make this war end?

This same war continues beyond history-
Beyond whispers, wisdom, or memory;
Bouncing between countries
And fresh, stubborn minds.
The same war
Going all the way back
To the beginning.

We are here as a host
To be forgiven
By the parasite-
We invited inside.
Worship the survivors
Of the front lines.
Imitate them-
Or kill them off
If they divide the will
Of the tribe.
But, this is the lie-

The playbook we live by is pride
While trembling to hide.
Together, we were beaten into submission
Yet, no one may absolve you-
No one may command you to kill:
You, alone, must learn to disobey
If you would rule your world without shame.

Off

I realized
I could fit my little world
Into a small bag
And disappear in the middle of the night.
It's harder than it sounds
In a story.

Everything seems to be holding on.
I could stay and bleed circles
And wrap stars all around me
Into spells-
And convince myself
To obey.
Obsess over the spectacle of death
And create a womb
Of its intent,
Or look away.
Even the pace-
Every step is another world away
And these greetings
Are the everlasting oaths
Of free form.

Realize-
What we have
May not last.

If that is the path,
Then forget the past;
Recognize this new life
Or make it up
Along the way.

Leave the shadows
To the suffocation of light;

Rest now
In the shade.

Name

This sun is our every season.
There will be no other invitations,
And there will be no light tap
On the shoulder
For sad goodbyes.
If we could put the whole thing on the scales
We'd see that evil
Carries exactly the same weight
As the righteous, in hate.

Where the barbs are now indiscriminate
And inevitable,
They are small and mundane;
The same
As emotions-
We ask them to find sunlight in the rain.

There were oceans of frozen fields
And abandoned terrain,
Untouched by fickle gods-
They make absurd demands
And they complain.
Have you witnessed the will
Of the self-righteous,
And the dementia, frozen upon the plains?

But, know this:
I will carry you
As far as I am able-
When I cannot go on,
We will stay.
I will never quit.
I will never walk away.
We can go to the end together,
Then, be forever on our way.

Ghost Town

In the crumbling brick castles
And back alley schools,
The madmen and fools
Besiege themselves.

These are toe holds-
My same stepping stones-
Inscribe new letters upon them;
Create words
To replace a language of slang.
I use them to separate
The things I know
From everything I can never hold together.
These words are my last hiding place.
The only way you will ever find me.
One by one,
We slip away.
Each of us-
Alone- will face the storm.
Alone, I call for the rain.
It comes to hide me
And keeps the impending world at bay,
But, only for a little while.
Upon me, it comes to bear-
A beginning,
Gathering form somewhere-
Behind the same dark realm.
We were told there was one Father.
I found a feminine deity there, instead.
Another station
On the crucifix of dread,
When, to simply carry on, was our only intent.
Accidents unwound,
And purpose was found-
Always, a step behind where I thought I should be,

And just in time
To see it all fall apart.
Now, that the windows are boarded-
All defenses shored,
The storm dissolves into myth
And failure into lore-
This hammer, the anvil,
And the sword.

Baggage

Whatever you thought of a soul
May stop with the heart
Or drift happily forward
With our invisible,
Whimsical inventions.
When bored,
We can decorate the empty space
With crayons, charcoal,
And cover ourselves with paint.
Understand the war cry, and the dancing drought, for rain.
Everything was forgiven
Simply, so it could be forgotten.
But, it never ends this way.
Redemption cannot be given,
It must be taken.
When it becomes too heavy
I leave it behind
And try to double back
If I remember, and the world gives me time.
Somehow, life reclaims everything
I try to lose,
But I know it won't end this way.
I pick these things up-
Think about them again
And through will
Invent a way down-
A way through promises I made.
Claw through the dirt-
Through the other side
Of the earth,
Disappear into the crowd.
Only you will ever know me.

Halo

We live under the protection of rare atmosphere
And within the envelope of the sun.
The elements have watched over this family
Since we crawled toward answers,
Asking,
Always asking.
Whenever we grow weak and soft
We are given this hard lesson:
These worlds owe us nothing-
One day there will be nothing left to take.
The bloody water illusion
Of blue green algae
Stains the stones uncovered along the shore,
The pyramids-
Above us and before.
The moon perfectly covered the sun,
And now, there is a crown of thorns.
Prophesy is a pattern-
Recognition, a sign
Given as a gift
From the old Gods,
As shortcuts through time.

And there will always be new gods.
They surround us, the ones who listen.
We build new altars on the old holy ground,
But the cast and crew
Seems to stay the same.

Everyone is here
For the final incarnation
Of planet earth.
We will deconstruct the coliseum-
Strip everything bare
To build ships

And start across the ocean,
Or the expanse of endless sky.
The sun
Is our halo,
And the planet is our ride.

Belief

The mind is sown
And scattered
By handfuls-
Reaching for other things.
The never ending task
Is the cultivation
Of efficient weeds.
The vines climb by crack
Into growing maps,
Rolled and lashed to an ax-
The legend, the lash-
A language we cannot read yet.

I make no choice
As to what survives me.
I divide provisions
To withstand the siege-
A common theme
To the royalty of paranoia.
Repetition marks time
And the incantations
Beg for belief, yet only love cannot lie.

The evidence is all around us,
Gathered by scavengers
With the patience
Of our empirical replacements:
Everything is done
But the deed.

On the road at night

Another stop
To examine the state
Of the road.
Kill the engine,
Kill the lights.
Hold your breath and listen.
Hear the insects pulse
And keep time
As every dark stretch
And every path in the past
Closes in.

A summer wind
Will push for a simple way out,
But there is nothing left to barter
And no way left to trade.
The road is too rough
And too fast by day.
And with no reason to sleep
There is no reason
To wake,
And only the roads leading away
Seem to understand this place.

Camp

The ocean stops for nothing.
On shore we divide ourselves
Between stages of hope and grief.
We make fires
With whatever we can
And make camp
With anything we find along the beach,
Buried in the sand,
And outlining the recent wrecks, by relief.
Fading flags of the past are flown,
And their holes
Are patched and sewn
With fishing line,
Found in great tangles
Between the rocks
And growing reeds.

The children are tamed
By little castles,
With moats draining into the sea.

This life,
Beyond four walls,
Will not tolerate
The stranger
Who does not speak.
The sleepless black figure
Moves through the back of our minds-
The magician
Is the outlaw,
The tower of dreams.
Not everyone is alive
Amongst us,
And some may never die.
No hero is coming to save us

From our own lives,
Or a single thing
We left behind.
By morning, the fires have burned to nothing,
And the tide
Has swallowed the castles within reach.
Do you go on, or go back, and dig up your old beliefs?

Grace Street

We buried the ghosts
We created as childhood friends
In a hole
Behind the house
I grew up in.

The town shrinks
To its true size
By following
The cracks in the street.

Imagination is adventure,
And the kids running by
Become laughter-
Lost animations
And outlines climbing trees.

Jump
Into a simple
State of being,
And the future
Is caught in the breach,
Between the world-
Then-
And the world
Beneath our feet.
To follow this world,
Is to sacrifice all childish things
That we might finally
Be free of peace.

The Archetypes

The shapes
In the imaginations
Of shadow
Chase harmless creatures
Into desperate corners.

There-
Surrounded,
They are driven to defend themselves,
Along with everything
And everyone else.
They survive by invention
And by reluctant violence, remain free.

They, of dark shadows
Defy preconceived answers
And the traps
On trails in the forest.
They rise
Taking shape out of love, vengeance,
And the marching of this machine.

Their eyes shine
With a flash of light and glow in the night-
Something the sight has in common.
They always come-
They always listen,
And they ask me to tell
The same story of time.
This was earlier,
When we knew
That we are connected to living creatures
By heart and mind-
How the evil inflicted upon them
We consume and solidify.

We have all been here a thousand times,
We have all known each other before-
Now I have reminded you-
And you will begin to remember more.

Harbingers

The spirits
Team with disobedience.
Ask the phantoms
To enter
The arteries,
These entrails-
Divine portents
And prophecy
To induce meaning,
Making worlds
Of this pile of blood, flesh, and guts-
Then, twisting it all into some kind of luck.

A little ship
Of what we had,
What we could be,
If only we surrendered –
If only we could invite rebellion,
By retreat.

Along the edge,
Inside-
The body is tied
By the accusations
Of the faithful-
Dead infections and negative entities.

So, they burned them-
And they said it set them free.
Any infraction an agony
And original becomes a freak.

There is no name in betrayal,
No loyalty in fear-
Whispering to yourself the things you must speak,

That no other may ever hear.

Volunteer

I remember the laughter
Bouncing back and forth
Between the high walls
Of the valley.
Though the mountains
Are seen
As obstacles to surmount,
Or conquer for high ground-
Above the plains,
With a river carving further down.

The sun rises and sets
So close together,
We live like the weeds-
Sprouting between the cracks
In random magic and unlikely abstract math.
Those of us, once dormant,
Will rise-
Fighting with the mountains
For sunlight,
Flooding in the spring.

We will gather ourselves together-
We will master the current,
We will ride the wave.
We will create a purpose
Even by these short days
Winding down.

These knots in the grain,
Where, cut to the roots
Once again,
Grows this muscle memory,
And resolves itself with rage.
You have eyes but cannot see-

And something like an echo
Where love, itself, should to be-
That seed-
The salvation
Of immortality.

She

All around us
Are loose ends,
Forgotten where they lay.

They are in the low tones
Of conversations
Left behind
And whispered
When prayers
Were pleas.

There are miles ahead
To travel-
And for all that matters-
We decide to leave.
I saw nothing was resolved,
But, why would it be?
And I wish I could forget
The way you can forget
About me.
But it's all over now;
Every sharp word
Tucked away
Like broken glass-
Artifacts,
In the landfill
Of history.

Advent

The unspeakable things
Become the most persistent memes-
Echo into action,
By lack of satisfaction, title,
And theme.

The interesting thoughts
Always manage to flee;
Born of mad pursuit-
And the constant invitation
Of chains.

Something in the shadows
Is always willing
To take shape,
Make reservation of mind-
Take payment
For proof of life,
And fail to honor the trade.
Sensing the long, empty handed walk home
With the idea
That evil is a free for all-
That fatigue of conscience,
Felt every step along the way,
Is impossible to map
In this terrain.
This good and gracious pestilence
Is the impetus
To set the world on fire,
And hope to be forgiven
Some day.

Winter

The darkness
Was always easy enough
To disrupt.
The echoes
In the wake of footsteps-
Fade,
Into irreverent bits
Of conversations made-
Grateful
To honest laughter,
Itself-
Holding hands,
Arms around shoulders,
And guided by the small of the back.
Meeting eyes
Gather together in arms.
Taking your breath away-
Inflating the night.

Empty life,
As if it were so simple,
Silent-
Winter white;
When the lights of the little towns
Go off
And the moon is cold and bright.

The Burning Village by the Sea

Ahead, smoke distorts all dimensions
Of distant grey clouds,
Bending the light itself
Through this lens, as energy.
It expends itself into the sky,
And when the sun sets
Little dots of flame guide me
To the first island
Opened by fire.
Below the village
The salt water sweat
Guides by this future of fear.

By dawn the destruction becomes clear
And complete,
As if everything I've fled
Stands before me again,
And each of my flaws
I am forced to see, vividly.
The will to live
Stands behind a crowd
Like the forest
Hiding within trees.

Bear witness to all-
Accept, even if you cannot believe,
That the paradise of mankind
Is undone
By greater design
Than that within me.
So, go on-
You can bring it with you
But you cannot have peace.

Everything

The vision I recognize
Is strewn with weapons-
Acquired by deliberate devices
And twisted minds.
Survival is by intention
Defense- by alchemical,
Mathematical sequence, and ignorance of organic life.
And luck-
I have learned to create by the number of my name.

There are bodies buried in the sand,
Covered by wind and the waves.
They take a collection
By decomposition;
They are devoured by invisible
Microscopic means.
With time and the tide
They return us to the sea.
With this I hear them speak:
Go on,
Don't wait for me;
Though I watch, I wave,
Knowing tomorrow
Is an aftershock of today,
And after awhile
The voices of the dead
Will fade-
It isn't in their interest to stay.
The future is turning pages,
Slowly,
Pasting pictures
Between the paragraphs
In fits of patience,
Pushed away.
Nothing stays buried

In the sand.
Nothing stays washed out to sea.
It all comes back
Eventually.

The Origin of Sin

I've seen all
I was intended to see.
All is nature-
All surrounds me.

When belief
Becomes a quiet servant
To the madness
Of its master,
Murder is amnesty.

They tell me
Faith
Is forgiveness
For the sin
Of humanity.
Live the lesson
Over and over again
Until your heart
Barely beats
Beneath the scars.
Put down a life's worth of guilt
Beside a life's worth of shame.
Though, it wasn't yours to carry,
You've shouldered all the blame.
It's been easier to accept,
Than to explain
Or walk away.

Tack and Trade

Between the tide
And the trade wind,
I am carried along the coast.
For so long
I've fought against the forces
Of this world;
Always going in the opposite direction
Until I was exhausted
By ignoring the signs.
I put a fist
Into the water
And pull the ocean behind me.
I open my hand in the water
And steer myself-
Easily off and back on course.
The direction of fate,
Following a few fingers,
And by direction-
Retaliate.
Forward-
Far,
The great solar temple
Drops below the earth
And leaves the sky in flames.
By fire we make offerings-
By sacrifice,
Without blood-
But, I didn't bother
To say goodbye-
I don't want anyone
To remember my name.
So, tack into the wind
And scatter the past
Into the wake.

Death and I

The unsettled water ahead
Seems to have swallowed a war
Intact,
And boiling
By disasters past.
This is everything
I've learned to forget,
Coming to the surface.
The tyrant wind
We all face
To find the dread of dying
Worth the fall from grace.

Stow the sail.
Secure the supplies-
Tie yourself to the mast
And smile.
This is what you've known
All along.
Fear is the rumor-
You started it yourself.
The lighthouse,
A beacon
To the sharp rocks,
And the rock to a wellspring.
From spring to sea, thus salvation will be-
Immune to myself-
The storm.

The shore- civilization,
Death and I-
The horde.

The Coming Revolution

I navigate by the stars
And try to sleep
Through the heat of day-
Find I'm happier this way,
Contending with the darkness
Directly,
Along the edge of this new age.

I'm not the only one.
Alone, in the middle of the ocean
I can hear
All the little fears
As they arc like sparks
Between the ruts
We have worn through worry.

The great change is here.

Many will not survive,
Or even try;
Denying this new reality
For the comfort
Of reflex and the routine deaths
Of someone else.
We've been raised on entertainment this way.
Now, hear their prayers
Through the floor boards
And the cellar doors
Nailed shut.
Cross yourselves if you must.
The end of this age will not be stopped.

Cocoon

Moving west
Seems to make way
For the womb
Around which I've cobbled this invention.
The future-
Dead center,
Is a gift I wrapped long ago
With trinkets of this life inside,
While I, myself-
Was out of mind.

More long stretches
With short, incomplete memories
To fill in-
Failing sentences
Of weak words,
And time served-
So few are second chances
And threadbare along the seams.
Following the constellations
I notice
They are no longer
Where they used to be.
And I know it won't be long
Now that the earth
Is catching up with me.
If I can live in this body,
If I can live with this brain-
By self destruction,
If I survive
This circumspect game;
A half breed,
Blinded by faith
So far along the way.
If I can live,

I may find out why
Someday-
Within this cocoon of spiders web
And venom
In my veins.

Becoming

Creatures
I've neither heard of
Nor seen
Surface through the sea
To inspect me.

Nocturnal
Through the hunted night
Myself-
A stranger
And friend against doom,
Having placed myself before it so often.

These strange things descend
And I am abandoned
Right where I began
When I entered the wilderness, alone.
The lost time of having gone no where
With the transparent wings
We used to believe in;
They carried us around the room.

When I close my eyes
I leave.
I need nothing to breath
Beneath the surface of the earth-
Below the water and up in space-
Below the surface of the sun,
And in the reflections
Of everyone.
Everyone who ever lived-
Everyone who ever died-
Is a part of this planet
We are leaving behind.

It is harder to be happy.
It takes forever
To say goodbye.

Little Wooden Ships

Standing alone
Becomes many things;
I must see many times
Before I understand what they mean.
Watching the sun
Put twelve thousand years
In their place,
While the perfect bookend
Bleeds away.
On this empty plateau
I recognize-
Through time- signs
Hidden before my face
Squandering so much life,
Carving my weak purpose
Into the existing cracks
Of crumbling civilization.
I tell little lies about hope,
But I wanted in on the riot.
I wanted to pile these carefully shaped stones
From the foundation
Into a feral lair
Of the wild.
We will revert to hunting in packs.
And we did,
Until it all collapsed.
Again,
I salvage the planks-
Weathered,
With rusting square nails;
It's narrow
And solid enough now
To attach the sail.
A little wooden ship
Built around a bottle.

Dead or alive-
All that's left of the message is the messenger inside.

Altar

Somewhere in the forest,
An altar was found.
All that was lost
Was awakened-
The intimacy
Of inexplicable gods-
Always silent.
They listen
Without demand
Without comment-
Understand-
All the details
Forgotten by man.
Out of fear of what we will find.
If I have the eyes to see
And the ears to hear
What is inside.
See the wind
Through the waves-
The whitecaps- fractals,
Arrive like the sense
Of soft breath while sleeping.
Slow your heart,
Extend your brain;
Becoming who we are,
May shape this world
Just the same.
Through the window,
By the moon,
By the tidal locked planets
Our system invades-
Casting Titans every which way
With the remains of ancient civilizations
And gravitational waves.
Saturn

Was the twin
Of Jupiter,
Before this binary system could escape;
Held together
By invisible forces
And through shallow
Unmarked graves of cataclysmic change.

Keystone

Sleep
While the photographs fade.
Liquid,
Like fingers
Through the memories,
And memories-
Leak through brain waves.
The universe
Quickly fills the cracks
In the worlds around us,
Expanding above and below,
Contracting within.

This is where we dig.
This is where we find the clay
And mix the mortar.
This is how we stuff the cracks
Of the past.
This is the color of blood,
And with blood
We temper the blade.
Gathered around the fire
And the forge we create-
This is where we cast shadows,
Hammer the crowd
Around the anvil
And overtake these dreams
Of sound and power-
The music
Of synchronicity-
Insane.

Fading Away

The dark clouds
Gather like a conscience
And scatter
With apologies.

They return,
Making new runs
Along the weak spots
Until vengeance
Is worn down
Into tired forgiveness.
The sky
Doesn't remember why it is fighting
With water and light.
There is nothing left to say
And the sun doesn't seem as bright
As I remembered it to be
When I was a child.
It sets
Without being seen
From the shore-
Absent and bored.
Wandering away
To battle windmills
With rain.

Nomad's Land

The survivors
Will be the people of the forest.
They will explore the proud towers
Of triple paned
Bullet proof glass,
And make time
Along the spillways,
And through the cultivated concrete frames.

There are patches
And paths
Of wild grass
Like redemption
Reaching our of every crack.
The wilderness gives,
And the wilderness takes it back.

Wagons, pulled by horses
Will rattle along what is left.
Along the old highways
They will camp,
And in the median
Between lanes.
These are the cities of those who wander-
Lost tribes retracing the past to impact.
The castles are constructed
To be seen crumbling-
They are waiting in their jungles,
Until then.
The red eye blinks in the sky-
The winged serpent
Crossing back and forth
Across the continent,
Belly stuffed
With the hunt.

The past
Has always gone too fast-
Given, to get another day.
And another day we wander with fate.

Creating The Calendar

Islands are everywhere
Along the way-
The only thing to punctuate the days.

The same villages
Are made of mud bricks
And sticks-
And better things to do
With sunny days.

The trees
Are pillars pushed from the earth,
Holding us up
And out of the reach
Of our enemies.
There are so many ideas
Of heaven slipping by,
As forgettable as mild weather
Beside the struggle
To survive.
These Islands
Are the triage
Behind a daydream,
Separating the living
From the dead
And from the dead-
Further dying-

As this world
Becomes the next.

How I Came To This Place

The columns
Carved out of stone
Seemed to be a better way
To defend the cave.
The civilized will
Before the wilderness;
Appearing to be strong
Where we are weak.
The familiar things,
And their impressions-
Far from our true home-
Despite the story we tell today.

Would I know
If all were lost?
Would I feel
An emptiness
In the air?
Does the wind
Become the breath
Of all living things?
Am I truly the last
In that long line
Of the past,
Or does the future
Pull us all
Farther away?

Muscle Memory

The only mark
Upon the sail
Is a world wrapped in thorns,
Twisted
Into a bloody wreath.
Into the bow
And the stern
Is a small iron knife
Chiseled in relief.
The patina stain
Of rust,
Our earthly blood brother-
From the first sacrifice,
We filled this well
With ink.

From the first fire
To the final battle-
The soldiers are all dead,
And the prisoners
Have been set free-
Delivered by destiny
If that's what you want to believe.
But, it all seems
Like an accident to me.

The survivors
Walk away
With whatever they can salvage-
Whomever they could save,
And what ever slipped into the fray.
This is the blood,
Born of fire
And muscle memory, deranged.

The Fire and the Flame

All of the exceptions exhale-
Shapeless,
Startled awake
By imperceptible changes
And lulled back to sleep
By the heartbeat.
Putting stone
To seed
We bake bread
For the multitude to eat.
Putting stone
To steel
We bring our world to heel,
And grant the oracle
Our burnt offerings.
What blame can we place
Upon the gods
We have imposed upon mankind?
We've made everyday
The same,
Where imagination must escape.

Banished
To the top of the mountain
In the shadow of a cave-
Are they who tend the fire
Through the weight
Of their own shame.
The stories are almost identical,
With different places
And different names.
In a cave up on the mountain
Are the keepers of the flame.
It is the light of salvation

And civilization, the same;
A light- like liberty-
And life itself to blame.
You will lose everything you cannot fight to defend,
So, you just walk away
With everything you wanted to say, in silence.

The Gate

Because love grows
Like the roots of wild grass-
Shorn close to the ground-
Trampled by the great herd
Of reality.
We plow
And plant straight rows
Where the meek
May run and hide.
See the difference
Between living in the sunrise
And running
With the predators of the night.
Between the meticulous cultivation
Of love and its loss,
We eat ourselves alive.
Let the world track you down
Once in awhile.
Let them take you by surprise.
Every step is toward ruin,
And your creation is inside.

The Entity

War is the ghost
Watching over your shoulder,
Whispering in your ear.
Half of the earth
Lives within its own shadow
At any given time;
The eclipse in observation
By our blind side,
And half of ourselves
Doing anything possible
To hide.
Will the next battle
Be our signature
Upon the world?
Is this where we sign up
For the afterlife,
Or opt out-
Carrying, instead,
The same stone
Up the everlasting mountain,
Stranded by weather
Beyond the pass.
I see the walls
Fall around me
Without explanation
Or apology.
Is life your servant,
Or you its slave?
This is how we separate the living
From the dead.

The Chief Cornerstone

There is dawn,
There is dusk-
All the same
By this delivery
Into a walking sigh
Of sleep-
Teaching a feather to fly.
The hollow bones,
Descended of unknown giants
And the Leviathan
Of legendary deep.
Now, circle around me,
Flutter, my little bird-
Little me, this certainty-
That I am where
I was meant to be:
A single cell
Beside the cornerstone
And the Titans
Of creativity.
If the world
Were a womb
And sky the seed,
Might I slip away
By the manifestation
Of the storm
Upon the sea.
The way through
Is the way out.
And the only possibility.

Memories of Prison

Give birth
To the edge of evolution.
Benign mutations
To all those
On the outside.
This is the tempest
Of peaceful lives
And the double edge:
The entire length of the blade
Hanging over every head.

Who fathers this horde of fear?
Who abandons the future
To the back alleys
And the world
Beneath the streets?
Here, the last to learn
Has the farthest
To throw away the keys.

These are the steps:
Small, insane circles
Under artificial, constant light.
There is nothing
To hide the lines-
Soften the mistakes.
Everyday is another duel within mind,
Constructing perfect prayers:
I've given up the wish to die young-
The suffering was satisfied
With time
And no one could be more surprised.

Ultraviolet

Open and exit vermillion-
This blood
For that blue sky
This dawn
For the twilight
Of the Gods.

This universe bleeds
The ultraviolet,
Liquid, carbon sea.

Recite your dreams to me,
While I sleep
This monster of creation,
Only I would call a home-
Grown to those same stepping stones
Of the past
And repeat.
Only your sins belong to you.
We were tricked, carrying the burden
Of generations
Before we even learned how to speak.
Drop them now
At their feet.
This life is all you have to bargain with.
You don't have to believe them
Because you listen patiently in practice.
Remember: love has always been kind.

The Mend

Over a long winter
We cannibalized the past-
Presently horrified
By the path
Our descendants
Will come to despise.
If anything can be salvaged
The instincts we hand down
May be worthwhile.
The savage tools
We've never had to use
Are sharp
And safely packed away.
Sometimes, there are mistakes.
These trails are hacked
Out of the wilderness
Along dead end tracks, the marrow of bones boiled and cracked-
The landscape is noted
And samples stowed away.
We may come back some day.
We may see nothing untoward, contrived, or pre-arranged.
The breaking of bones
And the sorrow consumed
In grey matter-
In pots of baked clay
With watercress, wild roots, and decay.
What we cannot use
Will be buried
With the primitive tools
And the four winds
Out on the plains.
Something haunts
The old forests
And will never go away,

Whether we remember
Or we forget,
The hole in the forest-
The trapdoor in the stage.

Helvetica

The Archetypes act
As invocations
Of the great storm.
The descending footsteps
Of destruction-the Titans and the form.
Shooting stars lean into the atmosphere
And clear a path for new life;
Eons in space
Exalt upon solid ground,
Granting our pillars to horns
And the window in the canopy, a scene of our time.

Dystopian heartbreaks
Do not come out as romantically as ancient promises.
Pick a chapter,
Pick a verse;
Choose the interpretation
Of your favorite curse.
And give it to bold block graffiti
No one will ever read.
Imagine the Vatican
As a wonderful museum
Of confession,
And mankind-
Victorious in final form-
Invincible.

Only now, after all else has failed,
And our evil dreams
Have finally run their course,
Can we succeed.
I always knew I was the outlaw,
Sent to stop an evil seed,
Camouflaged in absolution,
In trust, and deceit.
So many men
Are hiding and dressed up as priests
Speaking in tongues
Without the memory of medicine
And the sacred
In the deed.

The Hanged Man

These great things
Are grown from small seeds.
What reaches
Over the side of the boat
From the dark
And the deep-
From oblivion,
I've so far
Refused to see.
But I've noticed
The long shadows of deception-
Salvation
Is a common disguise,
So soft,
When you want to scream.
What is the price
For refusing to contend with this?
Without so much as an argument,
So many will feed the shadows
With their young,
Bait the waters,
Salute the flag
And cheer the beast on.

Surrounded by an ocean,
I drowned
Within my little ship,
I declare-
I decree-
This life goes on without me.
This is the map we leave
And the luck we try to pass
Through our sins
And beyond our grief.

The Buoyant Below

I open my eyes
Under water
And I see
The degrees of separation
Between living on land
And returning to the sea.
The deeper I go,
The easier it becomes
To breath.
The darkness
I had imagined
Coming from below
Was leaking from within me.
And illumination-
A warm direction of mind,
Pointing where I intended to be.
Is something
Outside of myself-
Waiting for me to listen;
Waiting until now
To speak.
How many times has mankind
Retreated into the water
To survive?

There is no going back this time.

At the Edge of the World

This entity and I
Built our lives
Like a bunker
Waiting for an attack
I knew would never come.
So, I stepped outside
And prayed for one.

There was a long
Unbroken line
Back to the last Rosary beads I've seen.
Have I ever
Expected an answer?
I have hoped
To be proven wrong
When the nights were long
And empty.
There is the urge to keep looking
Behind me,
At the impressive stage set,
And the dread-
Knowing the curtains
Will never fall.
The players believe
They are their characters
And improvise it all.
The lights go down
When it's time to hunt
And come up
When it is time to hide.

Uniform

The steady kill
Keeps a village alive-
All hands high
Through good times-
When the monuments burn brightly
And expire.

Thereafter,
They gather around the same stories,
The same tame fire.
The crops are grown
In failing rows
Of ash and inertia.
Harvest goes by in the rain
And reaps the idle brain-
By curse;
This is an accident of birth,
Fate, and the cold calculations
Of hate.
But, who is to judge
Without the strength to lift the scales
Or the courage
to counter its weight?
Our intention
Is the flawless execution
Of Latin mass
And the exaggerations
They create.
At one time
The offering of flesh and blood
Was known to be black magic.
Do you partake
Or leave this behind?
Is this necessary to survive?

In nomad's land
To face the future,
You must first turn away
From the past.
These are the things we've known for so long
We've forgotten at last.

The State

With so many broken chains,
We will have
Our brief slave state.
Pass the hat.
Send away for the jet empire
Before they stake their claim.
Our parents and grandparents
Signed us up in foreclosure
When the print was too fine
To explain.
So, how do you fight
A satellite guided, multiple munitions missile
With our collection of sticks and stones?
And you could say
Their feast was a success-
They devoured their own children
Before they were even born,
For a taste
Of an imaginary
Retirement home.

Maybe we will see you next year
Around summer
If it's possible
To get away.

Eye Of Saturn

Eye of Saturn
Eye of the Moon-
Ask a shadow
To describe the shape
Blocking the sun:
Contempt.

The key is the treasure,
You collect along the way.
You pick up the pieces
In the meantime,
Put them back together
For the chance to scatter them
Once again.

The New Planet

As for the dead,
I can hear them
Saying goodbye.
They say it over and over again.
They think I cannot hear them, though I listen to only one.
We move through Mars, my invisible sun,
To Her I listen, to Her I speak.
The islands become planets
And we move past solar systems,
Unmapped and unchained
And immense orphan bodies
This life cannot explain.
Black is the primary cxpansc;
By the absence of near objects reflecting light,
And the charge field of the universe,
Follows hunger and failure.
It overwhelms philosophical debate.
The end of this suffering
Means the survival of the world is at stake.
But, it won't come our way this early in the game.
There are too many corners where the cannibals can hide,
Preserving themselves insane.

When I see I cannot stop-
When I've come too far to turn back-
I will plot my course
For the center of the closest sun.
I will see what this life has left
And if I can send something back to explain.
I've been close enough to madness,
And seen enough to despise cruelty.
I've seen all hope broken
On the rocks
With the solid bits
Of skill

And collapse
At long last:
Oblivion, I survive.

Meridian

The days and nights
Have conspired to hide answers from me.
The simplicity of navigation by the sun
Has bled into the constellations,
And on a clear night,
So far from man made light,
I can see the one true map in the stars.
Communion
With our ancestors
Comes along the zodiac,
And the crux between the earth
And the sky.
I am much less alone
With these houses;
Each step of Horus,
Each hour of the day, the maddening flock in chorus.
By Set, the steps of night are silent behind the sun,
Exchanging the sharp light of planets
As if some were on urgent business,
And others have secrets-
Without the means to explain what has begun.
Some have no heart left to hear the sadness of the story
Spoken out loud or carried upon cloven hooves.
The scratches where there are scars,
And sadness where silence takes its place-
Come back when the silence
Is written upon your face;
When the dynamic is understood,
The how and the why become the pace.
Success is our weakness-
Our inability to accept pain,
Is not that we cannot suffer it, but that we cannot leave it where we
found it;
So, we start it all over

And over again.
The circle is completion and the prophecy of the damned:
Outside the circle-
The morning star
I am.

Big Medicine

I work with whatever the wind
Will give me.
Some days
Are practical jokes
And the currents,
Above and below
Give another demonstration
Of practical expectations.
And I know the drill.
Most of my life
I've gathered big medicine;
And like weapons
These little bottles and jars
Carry a weight above and beyond their means-
Often more than it should be.
Even without wind,
We feel potential in the sky,
That everyday is a working day
And often
The work is the wait.
So, when the wind rises in my face
I steady my pace
And find like minds
Will bridge the gap
Between big medicine
The magician
And the magic of certain fate.
We walk the sky
And we start today.

Go

If there is any hope
For Almighty protection,
Look to it first from within-
And without these lonely thoughts-
Begin.

I've crafted my sword
From what was left
Of my shield,
And defense-
From a plastic storefront display.
Tired tracks
From the old world
Which only betray my path.

What kind of Hell
Heaven must be-
To keep dragging its creation
Back into its cage-
Limping the same promises along,
Swapping the same stories
Of paradise
For rage.

I now listen to the new world
Within.

Post Traumatic

We could talk about the difference
Between flyover dots
And the longing for death
And I-
The diatribe
Of life in the Midwest divide.
These are the scattered states;
How I got here,
And why I come back to the same place
Whenever I am away.
Fantastic, post traumatic-
In an electric light slap
And a flicker you could not have seen
Out of the corner of your eye.
The Golem-
The ancient grey,
And the reminder
Of abduction and the big break
From everything this world contains.
Not to see this odd beast,
But to see it so often,
In such detail-
You begin to think of nothing else.
The elephant is the air I breathe-
Is not-
Could never be-
An enemy,
But another slave-
Smashed together by this inside out cage.
Know that I am
This Centaur,
This half creature-
Half mistake,
And grateful I turned out this way.

Fortuna

Death and I,
Indivisible-
Survive.
Honed as a wet stone
And by design
Of Fortuna
The Goddess of mind
And the future of the species.
Peace seems to pace itself
By the strength of its own poison-
The maze of poverty
And the chemical assault
Upon the brain.
The prospect of damage
Drives the civilized
Further and further underground-
Excavating vaults
In the renovation of last resort.
How long can we live without sunlight?
Is it the same
Of welcome?
And how long can I live without love?
Set adrift upon this-
The empty ocean-
Below the primordial cliff.
I see the challenge
And the grand design
Of continental, planetary divide.

One day,
We will grasp whatever is left
Of language
And explain the difference
Between what love was,
What it has become,

And everything this world can be.

Legend

Have you seen the earth
Without the oceans?

Have you seen the world
Without water?

How,
Why we have even survived?
And if you dig it
Dig it deeper-
Deeper down-
Until you come out
The other side.

Can you reconcile
The invisible sun
The moon
And the scars?

Become Her

The mask of midnight
Attacks
And the storm swallows the world of water.
These roads
Become rivers
And those rivers
Run through me.
The foreign has become familiar
And I know-
Back home,
The grass
Has grown over the graves
Of heartache.

I no longer try to remember
Who I was
Or whatever may have been my beliefs.
By surprise,
I dropped the weight
Of my little world
Before the river,
To find what lies
At the bottom of the sea:
Tiberius,
The hand of the Empress,
The heart of the king.

Crater and Creation

The forgiveness of the old Gods
Will be put off
Until they're just forgotten.

The amphora of fantasy
Will sink
To the sea floor
Disappearing with the ancient world
Just off the coast.
The cave will collapse
Upon the clay jars
And pictographs-
The implant of mystery
And time-
Into the shallow salty sea;
And the beautiful dead-
Was never a fantasy-
When she speaks she glows within me.
We belong to each other again
And darkness
I set free.

The Old Sun

Remote,
My satellite shelter
Orbits the shade
And shadow-
A forbidden master
Is made-
In memory
Of the black sun.

The Titans sleep,
Rattling the window panes
When dreams escape
Into this Garden of Eden,
Where the tallest old trees
Are razed.
Celibate,
They prophesize superstitions

And treasure the memory
Of the dead.
But, they are not dead.

Writing with Sticks in the Sand

Somewhere on land,
On a cliff
Is the boy I was-
The boy I grew up with.
We could stay here all night.
We have yet to find
A better home,
And the crisis
Always comes between four walls.
The boy spends the night,

Like many nights,
Beneath the tree
Re-arranging the method-
Following the blood through the brain.
I didn't ask anyone to die for me.
Send someone else the bill,
And nice try-
It's a great story-
Maybe some other time.
I'm on a cliff,
Under a tree.
I wave,
Something elemental
Answers me.
It has taken all this time
To shake it-
Trade it all back
For the quiet,
Universal outline
Tracing the lights in the sky.
Constellations rotate their stories
Through time;
They tell me
I'm off the hook-
I was never on it
To begin with.
It was all someone else's cage.
But I know
I've barely escaped.

The Spore

The answers to so many questions
Are found buried in the desert.
Beginning at the end,
As destiny-
Is compost
And energy,
Our symphony.
Our map is the legend
And the ink itself
Our deeds;
Our fruit
Is consumption
And self becomes the seed.
Intelligence in final form
Of spore and frozen space,
Rises from the ashes
And every aspect
Of prophesy.
Revelation-
The true extent of the damage-
Its own inverse adventure
Of mutant salvation
Consolidated into sterile fossils
By common dust and sand.
These cherished fruits
Of future survival-
Inoculated in the absence of sanity,
Multiply in logic.
This messiah-
I followed into the desert,
Assembled on the hilltop-
I am born of the final stand.

Sense

It is hard to argue
With insanity-
It is difficult to reason
With paranoia;
They make such perfect sense.
Virile paranoia-
With so many silken threads
And threats
To chase and weave into higher meaning
And interesting answers
To life chained to the wheel.
Base fear,
Ever present and practical
Is put to work
With worry.
Like all forms of life,
They go on
Until all the food,
All the fuel,
And every store of logic
Has been consumed.
Only when nothing is left
Are we allowed to come to our senses
And regret.
The truth is a master of disguise.
It wears elaborate costumes,
Slips into flawless conversation
And credible accents.
Only when stripped bare

Will it confess.
Only then,
Do I recognize my old friend.

I Started Out by Accident

Would you be lured back
Into the wild woods we explored?
Would we leave a trail of breadcrumbs,
Knowing it is only for the birds and the squirrels?

Are we silent?
Are we still?
Do we mistake the pounding of our heart
For the sounds of the world around us?

They cannot hear
What you hear.
They cannot see
What you see.
They explain:
All happiness is a razor,
And you-
The down payment
On pain.
So give it away.
The all
Becomes the giant step,
Inexplicable-
Ok?
Understand-
Known- was never my own.
I can come close to the figure
But I can never
Show you the math.
And the world is illuminated
Just the same.
The questions are in plain sight
Hidden among the answers
And protected
Only by the fear

Of hearing
What they have to say.

We are the Front

We were born
Behind enemy lines,
Though it took half our lives
To realize-
Who we are,
Where we are,
And become afraid.
We've re-designed guerilla warfare
For the modern day.

Draw the enemy into the open
With paranoia-
Always engage
The darker side
Of their brain.
This-
My gun catalogue collection,
And the encyclopedia
Of improvised munitions.
I've amended it for the common era
Of Cat 5
Instantaneous gratification
And layered disarray.
It keeps the king nimble-
Afraid.
The water in his veins
Becomes vapor-
Danger-
Left deranged.

There are too many twisted milestones
And black holidays.
So many,
I think we have earned
Our escape

From the front line crapshoot parade.
I've already made other plans.
I'm enacting them
Little by little
Each day.

Solar Minimum

The apex
Comes by accidental design.
The account,
The ledger-
Is the book of love,
And the legion
Is the number of all names.
The torus-
Is of energy and time-
And blood-
The new medium of exchange;
Dribbled out
Like the last steps
Through the snow
And into the new ice age.
Survive,
Become the next root race
And time,
Being time-
Will begin again.
There is nothing you can do
To stop it.
There is nothing you can say
To make it change.
It has always been this way,
And mankind
Was never meant
To stay the same.

Fast Forward

As so many before us,
We ask for mercy
From the flood.
All of those things I meant to do
But did not do.
All of those promises I made,
All those things
I meant to say.

These,
And all waters recede
To the intersections of time-
To like minds.
Stay,
And cast your net
Into the same sea
Of idle starvation,
And curse the heavens again.
Or leave-
Look for the answer
To what it all means.
This life
Is now a foreign shore-
I set my ships on fire.

The Darkroom

The entities I conjure
Have expired.
Those exits-
Missed memories,
Careless-
And kept to photo negatives
Inside self addressed,
Stamped envelopes
I send to myself
From the road.

We could shrug it on
Or off,
Without the need
To develop these things
Within dark rooms
And by the absence of light.
These memories
Are as welcome
As you are now.
Longing for some father-
Knowing
There will be no sun-
Only setting,
Overcast
And overrun.
This dark room
Is a second hand construct,
To keep our lost child awake,
Safe, and alive,
Within all of us.

In Between Lines

The stencils I use
For the letters
Are layered
In a timeline
Of paint.

But the colors
Cannot stand out;
They give instruction-
Lend grace.
And history
Cannot grab you,
It cannot pull itself
Out of the page.
There may be hints
About what direction
We should take,
And through these allegories-
Pay attention-
Find yourself
Upon the stage.

Space

Everything fits-
Everything is in its place.
We have come over land,
Over sea,
This first leg of the race.

Yet, we find ourselves
Further and further away.
As if the universe
Is running away from us
And mankind
Is a plague.

Like I've built my little ship,
We will make our way through space.
We will make ourselves worthy,
Of whatever we must face.

We will survive as humankind
When we give
More than we take.

The Hourglass

Solitude,
Is this finite scattering
Your final measure of sand?
The sculpture-
A disposable compass
And the hourglass makes demands.
Soon, the confetti stars
And cut out planets
Will point to a single destination,
Then collapse.
All things are recycled by the tide,
But the meteorite-
Magnetic,
Is worked into a knife.
It works the tide
Into the mountains
And the stones
Into smooth pebbles
And piles of fossilized diatoms,
Keeping the swarm at bay.
We've marked the doorways of the firstborn-
The messengers are on their way.
Tetragrammaton is the shape-
The word is the name,
And these are the chronicles
Of our new age.
Remember the fire of Vesta,
The great Mother without form.
Call upon the Roman gods
Of cruelty
Kindness
And civilization;
Know that we have come a long way.
Call upon Janus
When stepping through a gate;

The Lares, the Penates-
When we make a new home somewhere.
Someday-
We will all forget.
The universe will fall silent and still
And every word, every look
Will have the weight and the love it was meant to contain.

Procession

Stand below Taurus,
A gear of the galactic plane.

Place space
Between our violent leanings
And this humble halo,
This crumbling grass crown.

Lost and found-
The barbarian tribe
Does ebb and flow,
Wax and wane,
Kill-
And find itself slain,
Before the altar
Of hidden knowledge
And the imperceptible hand
Of fate.

But, I don't like to mention destiny.
I don't like to give it weight
It may not have in this world.
It is an invisible idea-
More formless whisper
Than a word,
And legions have been carried
To that grave.

Alone,
We ask for forgiveness
And we are forgiven.
Alone,
We are given a spark
We must all nurse into a flame
And protect
From a universe of rain.

Players

There is a different cast
Occupying the stage.
And I have no part
Of the larger play.
The same
Is for the scene
Passing by the window.
Once in awhile
It looks in.
The low light horizon
In silhouette
Makes the set,
And I am the scratches,
Scribbles in the margin,
And content
To outline the sketch.

By the will of the mob
These plots are sentenced
To certain death.
And it seems absurd,
But life is like that.
The end
Is much of what we contend with.

The crowd will nail the doors shut
And give us
What they get.
In this coliseum,
We are the circus
And by performance
Bake the bread.

The March

This world of yours
Is not the world of mine.
The wide scenes
Are never screened
From the higher plateaus,
To the toiling figures
Working the fields below.

We take what we are ready to receive-
Leave behind
The things you don't need.
Try to keep up
Before the trail grows over
And you can no longer follow
The lies they lead.

Can you forget
Without forgiveness?
Maybe,
If you burn that framed photo
Of hate.

This is the year zero.
It is time
They were all erased.

The Abacus

Humanity is the unidentified
Falling object.
You will feel the universe
Surround you,
Attempting to solve itself.
You may try,
But find you are unable to help.
There are billions of sparks
And the hive
Is too small
For the swarm.
Millions
By mistake,
And too many to partake
In even shares of the place.

The lord of the food chain
Never seems to die,
And the balance of potential
Just passes by,
Head down-
Hoping to find something to eat.

We are all a part
Of the final equation;
And our children, the same vibration
The great primate
Sees the last pattern
Slide across the abacus
Just a little bit too late.
We have only
Our moment in time-
So, would you love,
Follow loss,
Or lay waste?

The Great Escape

We will put the new world
Back together
In a better way,
Knowing the future
Will find itself
In a similar place.

We will erect monuments
To guide those behind us
And remind them
Of the way we came.
Point them away from kings
And top down rackets;
Away from parasitic religions,
Re-enacting the same pageant
With new lines
In the same play.

Maybe this time
We will discard belief
Entirely.
Make them prove what they say.
But it will be cumbersome
And eventually
We will have the same games.
We will need
An entirely new planet some day.
It's always the same kind of people
We have to escape.
Our kin
Are too kind to kill.
And we are leaving this place, anyway.

The Mother ship

Thunderheads above
Like inexplicable alien ships
Moored to our path
And pier-
Shape shifting,
Preparing for the jump.

We say our goodbyes
To the blind
And to love-
Cursing our own foolish minds.

For belief
I would stay.
But, I cannot stay-
Choosing a plot
And planning a grave.
Someday the headstones
Will pave a nice way
Back to the village,
When the names have eroded
And the engravings have faded into vague shapes.
When the world cannot say
What it means to say,
And the planet
Is a grave-
The ghosts will speak into my ear-
Somewhere She waits.
Awaken!
This is the new world,
And we can unwind all this hate
Along the way.

Keepers of the Flame

The earth
Has never been conquered
By battleships
Or steel.
History gives false impressions
Of mighty legions
And their salvation of civilization
For scraps.

In peace,
The world was taken
Long before that.
Held in trust
By the interpretations
Of stars
And the skill
Behind hand crafted
Little rafts,
Pulled barefoot up the beach.

Styx

There is always
A dangerous crossing
And a quest.
There is always a dragon
To fight
Vanquish
Or befriend.
A sword too heavy-
And a shield,
Too light.

Is it an accident
That I have come this way?
Does it matter,
If I make it to the right place?
Was the path too obvious?
Was the choice too easy?
Have I even tried
To get out of this cage,
Or did I make the most
Of being a slave?

I have a feeling
I am where I was meant to be,
But I'm not so sure
I know what that means.
It's not as simple
As it seems
To be a little piece
On a chessboard,
When it is so easy
To create a new game.

Trips

Apex-
I, by accidental design-
The only way to survive
Is to do so, first
In the mind.
Beside the beginning of the trail,
We can stand aside,
Turn to fight
Or hide.
The front is I,
As I am the night sky
Calling out from emptiness to absence;
Setting traps with love
To set free all I find.

The Sapling Raft Almanac

The sea
Will always be
Our shelter from the storm.

When the tide comes in
We row into the wind;
With the current we cast our net.
Our catch extends our sails
Further yet,
And our course is the blue curve ahead.
The new world
Is the next world-
The quest-
Is all I have left.
To this
The universe provides,
Below the island
As above
The planets rise.
It is thus we become the One Thing-
And make record of these replies.
Careful scratches-
Mark each loss
Upon the mast
Of this-
Our bundle of broken sticks-
The sapling raft almanac.